APOSTLES' CREED

ALISTER McGRATH
WITH DALE & SANDY LARSEN

6 STUDIES
FOR INDIVIDUALS
OR GROUPS

Life
Builder
Study

INTER-VARSITY PRESS
36 Causton Street, London SW1P 4ST, England
Email: ivp@ivpbooks.com
Website: www.ivpbooks.com

*Originally published in the United States of America in the LifeGuide® Bible Studies series
in 2016 by InterVarsity Press, Downers Grove, Illinois*
First published in Great Britain by Scripture Union in 2017
This edition published in Great Britain by Inter-Varsity Press 2018

British Library Cataloguing-in-Publication Data
A catalogue record for this book is available from the British Library.

ISBN: 978–1–78359–819–9

Printed in Great Britain by 4edge Limited

*Inter-Varsity Press publishes Christian books that are true to the Bible and that communicate
the gospel, develop discipleship and strengthen the church for its mission in the world.*

*IVP originated within the Inter-Varsity Fellowship, now the Universities and Colleges Christian
Fellowship, a student movement connecting Christian Unions in universities and colleges
throughout Great Britain, and a member movement of the International Fellowship of
Evangelical Students. Website: www.uccf.org.uk. That historic association is maintained,
and all senior IVP staff and committee members subscribe to the UCCF Basis of Faith.*

Contents

Getting the Most
Out of *Apostles' Creed*

It is difficult to explain Christianity to an outsider if you haven't thought about it much yourself. Christians do indeed trust in God—but we believe certain quite definite things about him and about the impact this belief must have on us as believers. The Apostles' Creed is an ideal starting point for this vital process of consolidating your grasp of the faith.

For more than a thousand years, Christians in western Europe knew the Apostles' Creed only in Latin. Its opening words are *Credo in Deum*, "I believe in God." The English word *creed* derives from that word *credo*. It is an attempt to summarize the main points of what Christians believe. It is not exhaustive, nor is it meant to be.

The earliest Christian creed seems to have been simply "Jesus is Lord." Anyone who made this declaration was regarded as a Christian. For someone to confess that "Jesus Christ is Lord" is to declare that Jesus is the Lord of his or her life. To recognize that Jesus is Lord is to seek to do his will.

As time went on, however, it became necessary to explain what Christians believed in more detail. The full implications of declaring that "Jesus is Lord" needed to be teased out. What did Christians believe about God? About Jesus? About the Holy Spirit? By the fourth century, the Apostles' Creed as we now know it had assumed a more or less fixed form; what variations did exist were slight, and these were finally eliminated in the seventh century. The Apostles' Creed is a splendid summary of the apostolic teaching concerning the gospel, even though it was not actually written by the apostles.

The Apostles' Creed was not the only creed to come into existence in the period of the early church. However, it is the oldest and simplest creed of the church. All Christian traditions recognize its authority and its importance as a standard of doctrine. To study the Apostles' Creed is to investigate a central element of our common Christian heritage. It is an affirmation of the basic beliefs that unite Christians throughout the world and across the centuries.

The Christian creeds had their origins as a profession or confession of faith made by converts at their baptism. Since then, they have served other purposes—for example, as a test of orthodoxy for Christian leaders or as an act of praise in Christian worship. In our own day and age the creeds serve three main purposes.

First, a creed provides a brief summary of the Christian faith. You do not become a Christian by reciting a creed; rather, the creed provides a useful summary of the main points of your faith. Certain Christian teachings are not dealt with in the creed. For example, in the Apostles' Creed there is no section that states "I believe in Scripture." The importance of the Bible is assumed throughout; indeed, most of the creed can be shown to consist of direct quotations from Scripture.

Second, a creed allows us to recognize and avoid inadequate or incomplete versions of Christianity. By providing a balanced and biblical approach to the Christian faith, tried and tested by believers down through the centuries, the creed allows us to recognize deficient versions of the gospel.

Third, a creed emphasizes that to believe is to belong. To become a Christian is to enter a community of faith whose existence stretches right back to the upper room in which Jesus met with his disciples. By putting your faith in Jesus Christ, you have become a member of his body, the church, which uses this creed to express its faith.

Many people have found their faith immeasurably strengthened and matured by being forced to think through areas of faith they would not have explored without the Apostles' Creed. See the creed as an invitation to explore and discover areas of the gospel that otherwise you might miss or overlook.

Think of how many others have recited these words at their baptism through the centuries. Think of how many others have found in the Apostles' Creed a statement of their personal faith. You share that faith, and you can share the same words that they have used to express it.

Suggestions for Individual Study

1. As you begin each study, pray that God will speak to you through his Word.

2. Read the introduction to the study and respond to the personal reflection question or exercise. This is designed to help you focus on God and on the theme of the study.

3. Each study deals with a particular passage so that you can delve into the author's meaning in that context. Read and reread the passage to be studied. The questions are written using the language of the New International Version, so you may wish to use that version of the Bible. The New Revised Standard Version is also recommended.

4. This is an inductive Bible study, designed to help you discover for yourself what Scripture is saying. The study includes three types of questions. Observation questions ask about the basic facts: who, what, when, where and how. Interpretation questions delve into the meaning of the passage. Application questions help you discover the implications of the text for growing in Christ. These three keys unlock the treasures of Scripture.

Write your answers to the questions in the spaces provided or in a personal journal. Writing can bring clarity and deeper understanding of yourself and of God's Word.

5. It might be good to have a Bible dictionary handy. Use it to look up any unfamiliar words, names or places.

6. Use the prayer suggestion to guide you in thanking God for what you have learned and to pray about the applications that have come to mind.

7. You may want to go on to the suggestion under "Now or Later," or you may want to use that idea for your next study.

Suggestions for Members of a Group Study

1. Come to the study prepared. Follow the suggestions for individual study mentioned above. You will find that careful preparation will greatly enrich your time spent in group discussion.

2. Be willing to participate in the discussion. The leader of your group will not be lecturing. Instead, he or she will be encouraging the members of the group to discuss what they have learned. The leader will be asking the questions that are found in this guide.

3. Stick to the topic being discussed. Your answers should be based on the verses that are the focus of the discussion and not on outside authorities such as commentaries or speakers. These studies focus on a particular passage of Scripture. Only rarely should you refer to other portions of the Bible. This allows for everyone to participate in in-depth study on equal ground.

4. Be sensitive to the other members of the group. Listen attentively when they describe what they have learned. You may be surprised by their insights! Each question assumes a variety of answers. Many questions do not have "right" answers, particularly questions that aim at meaning or application. Instead the questions push us to explore the passage more thoroughly.

When possible, link what you say to the comments of others. Also, be affirming whenever you can. This will encourage some of the more hesitant members of the group to participate.

5. Be careful not to dominate the discussion. We are sometimes so eager to express our thoughts that we leave too little opportunity for others to respond. By all means participate! But allow others to also.

6. Expect God to teach you through the passage being discussed and through the other members of the group. Pray that you will have an enjoyable and profitable time together, but also that as a result of the study you will find ways that you can take action individually and/or as a group.

7. Remember that anything said in the group is considered confidential and should not be discussed outside the group unless specific permission is given to do so.

8. If you are the group leader, you will find additional suggestions at the back of the guide.

1

I Believe

I believe in God . . .

The Apostles' Creed in Latin opens with the words *Credo in Deum*, traditionally translated into English as "I believe in God." While "I believe in God" could mean "I am of the opinion that there is a God," in fact, it is a much stronger statement. Faith begins, however, with the acknowledgment that there is a God. *Faith means assent.*

Christians don't just believe—we believe in *someone*. More accurate translations of "I believe in God" would be "I have confidence in God," "I put my trust in God" or simply "I trust in God." Faith is not merely believing that God exists; it is anchoring ourselves to that God and resting secure in doing so. Faith is the response of our whole person to the person of God. It is saying yes to God. *Faith means trust.*

Time and again, Scripture encourages us to think of our faith as a personal relationship with God. God has publicly demonstrated his commitment to us and love for us in the cross of Jesus Christ; he will not abandon us. Faith is our commitment to God, a joyful and willing self-surrender to God. *Faith means commitment.*

Faith and good works in no way exclude each other. We do not come to faith by doing good works, as if we could buy our way into the kingdom of God. But real faith naturally gives rise to good works. Faith is active, seeking to express itself in the way we live. *Faith means obedience.*

GROUP DISCUSSION. What do you think of when you see the word *believe*?

PERSONAL REFLECTION. Perhaps you have always been able to say "I believe in God," perhaps you have recently affirmed or reaffirmed that statement, or perhaps you cannot honestly make that statement. If your ideas about believing in God have changed, how and why did they change? If your ideas have stayed consistent, what has kept them consistent?

In both the Old and New Testaments, Abraham is a model of faith—that is, of believing. God called Abraham to go to a strange land to receive his inheritance, and Abraham trusted God and went. He believed, even in apparently hopeless circumstances. *Read Genesis 12:1-8.*

1. What took place between God and Abram (later renamed Abraham)?

2. *Faith means assent.* Abraham apparently knew very little about God when God called him. Why do you think Abraham chose to believe in this God?

3. What do you think most people in your culture mean when they say "I believe in God"?

4. Has it always been easy for you to say "I believe in God," or have you struggled with that statement? Why?

5. *Faith means trust.* Which of Abraham's actions indicate that he said yes to God when God took the initiative to speak to him?

6. What are some ways you have said yes to God?

7. *Faith means commitment.* What were some radical consequences of Abraham's trust in God, for himself and for his household?

Read Genesis 15:1-6.

8. Almost twenty-five years had passed since God promised to give the land of Canaan to Abraham's offspring (Genesis 12:7). At that point, why might Abraham have had reason to lose his trust in God?

9. How did God promise to show himself trustworthy?

10. For Abraham, what was the relationship between faith and righteousness?

11. *Faith means obedience.* In these two passages from Genesis, how do you see Abraham being obedient to God?

12. What would you say to someone who would like to believe in God but has difficulty overcoming doubts?

13. How would you like your belief in God to mature and deepen during this study and beyond?

Pray about specific areas of life where you need to deepen your trust, commitment and obedience to the Lord.

Now or Later

- In the book of Romans, the apostle Paul built a case for how God counts a person as righteous. Study Romans 4:1-5, in which Paul referred to Abraham and quoted Genesis 15:6.

- Abraham showed his belief in God through radical obedience. Consider ways that God might be challenging you to express your faith in some life-altering way.

- Faith is like an anchor, linking us with the object of faith. Just as an anchor secures a ship to the ocean floor, so our faith links us securely with God. Sketch an anchor fixed firmly in the ocean floor, with the anchor rope extending up to a boat riding on boisterous waves. Label the waves with difficulties in which the Lord has held you fast and kept you from drifting away or being shipwrecked. Above the waves write a prayer of thanks for the Lord's steadfastness and faithfulness.

2

God the Father

Isaiah 40:21-31

. . . the Father almighty, creator of heaven and earth.

Throughout Scripture we find analogies that point to God's ability to reveal himself in ways we can understand, using illustrations we can handle. These scriptural images of God are easy to visualize and remember, yet on further reflection they convey important and profound truths concerning God.

The statement "God is our Father" means that God is like a human father. In other words, God is analogous to a father. In some ways he is like a human father, and in others he is not. There are genuine points of similarity as well as genuine points of dissimilarity. Like all analogies, the analogy of God as *Father* breaks down at points. However, it is still an extremely useful and vivid way of thinking of God.

GROUP DISCUSSION. Think of a place in God's creation where you find yourself especially aware of his presence. It could be a particular location, a familiar sight, a work of art or the presence of another person. Why do you feel especially aware of God there?

PERSONAL REFLECTION. What comes to mind when you think of God as Father?

Any idea of God as an impersonal being or force is immediately discounted when we speak of God as Father. To talk about God as our Father is to speak of his authority and care, but it is also to speak of his creativity. We are here because God brought us into being. Everything we see in the world was created by God and belongs to God. The universe reflects the wisdom, power and majesty of the God who brought it into being. *Read Isaiah 40:21-31.*

---

1. Identify the questions posed in this Scripture passage.

How would you answer them?

---

2. If we didn't have access to the Bible, what would we know about God from the world around us?

---

3. This passage includes many word pictures, especially in verses 21-26. Taken as a whole, what do you think these word pictures are trying to convey about God's relationship with the created world?

---

4. Why does God urge human beings to "Lift up your eyes and look to the heavens" (v. 26)?

---

5. At some time or other, either out loud or silently, most people have made the complaint expressed in verse 27. Consider God's response to that complaint (vv. 28-31). What new perspective does it offer a person who feels abandoned by God?

6. The Apostles' Creed expresses belief in "God the Father almighty." Throughout this Scripture passage, where do you see evidence that God is almighty?

7. How is thinking of God as Father especially helpful in prayer?

8. When your prayers to your heavenly Father apparently go unanswered, how do you respond?

9. How would you help someone with very negative memories of his or her own father to appreciate the fatherhood of God?

10. Think of times you have felt weak and exhausted, whether physically, mentally or emotionally. How have you experienced God renewing your strength at those times (vv. 29-31)?

11. What are some examples of what it means to "hope in the Lord" (v. 31)?

12. Where do you need renewed strength and hope from your almighty Father just now?

Ask your heavenly Father to meet your needs in every area of your life. Thank him for creating and sustaining you in his love.

Now or Later

- Study Hebrews 12:1-13 to see how the loving discipline of God demonstrates his fatherhood.

- Study John 14:1-14 concerning Jesus' close identity with the Father.

- Make a point of taking time to gaze at the night sky, or if there is too much light in your area to see the stars, look at other aspects of your natural surroundings in the daytime. Even the most urban setting offers opportunities to see clouds, sunsets and green plants. What do these created things say to you about their Creator?

3

God the Son: His Identity and Birth

Philippians 2:5-11

I believe in Jesus Christ, his only Son, our Lord. He was conceived by the power of the Holy Spirit and born of the Virgin Mary.

It is generally thought that the Apostles' Creed represents an expansion of a very simple and basic confession of faith: "Jesus is Lord!" Christians have always insisted that there is something qualitatively different about Jesus that sets him apart from all other religious teachers or thinkers. There is a vitally close connection between the person and the message of Jesus. What Jesus did and the impact he made on those who encountered him make his message important. In Jesus the message and the messenger are one and the same.

GROUP DISCUSSION. What are the attitudes of a good servant?

PERSONAL REFLECTION. What other lords have you been tempted to honor besides Jesus? How has Jesus proved himself better than any of them?

If Jesus is just a man, a human being like the rest of us, he shares our need for redemption—in other words, he can't redeem us.

He is part of the problem, not the solution to it. On the other hand, if Jesus is God, and God alone, he has no point of contact with us. He cannot relate to those who need redemption. Jesus' humanity provides that point of contact. And so we arrive at the conclusion that Jesus must be divine and human if he is to redeem us. *Read Philippians 2:5-11.*

1. Taking this Scripture passage as a whole, what is the relationship between Jesus and God?

2. In what sense(s) could Jesus be said to have "made himself nothing" (v. 7)?

3. How could Jesus be called a "servant" (v. 7)?

4. Jesus the Son of God was "found in appearance as a man" (v. 8). For you, what is most remarkable about the fact that God was incarnate in Jesus Christ?

5. What are the reasons for the exaltation of Jesus (vv. 8-9)?

6. The name of Jesus is now "the name that is above every name" (v. 9). Think of several great human leaders of the past and present. How is Jesus greater than each of them?

7. Verses 9-11 are full of adoration of Christ. When have you felt yourself caught up in that kind of adoration?

8. Try to envision the worldwide worship of vv. 10-11. What does it look like?

What does it sound like?

9. How does confessing Jesus as Lord bring glory to God the Father (v. 11)?

10. What does it mean for you that "Jesus Christ is Lord" (v. 11)?

11. What does it mean for you that Jesus Christ is *your* Lord?

Offer prayers of adoration to Jesus as Lord. Praise his particular qualities as they come to mind, such as his power, his humility, his unchanging nature, his mercy.

Now or Later

- Study Revelation 5, John's vision of the majesty of Christ.

- As a group, write various praises to Christ on slips of paper. Arrange the papers in a reasonable order, perhaps moving from praise for his humility, suffering and death to praise for his resurrection, presence and power. Fill in any gaps with transition words. Then speak your newly created psalm of praise together.

- To set today's Scripture in its full context, study Philippians 2:1-4 and 12-18 concerning the practical implications of Jesus' humanity for believers.

4

God the Son: His Death and Resurrection

1 Corinthians 15:1-28

*He suffered under Pontius Pilate, was crucified,
died and was buried. He descended to the
dead. On the third day he rose again.*

Suffering is a mystery that causes anguish to many Christians. It seems to call the love of God into question. The suffering of Jesus Christ on the cross at Calvary does not explain suffering. It does, however, reveal that God himself is willing and able to allow himself to be subject to all the pain and suffering that his creation experiences. We are not talking of a God who stands far off from his world, aloof and distant from its problems. We are dealing with a loving God who has entered into our human situation, who became human and lived among us as one of us.

GROUP DISCUSSION. What are some typical responses to suffering?

PERSONAL REFLECTION. Has suffering (your own or someone else's) caused you to question God's love? If so, what help have you found from Scripture?

Jesus Christ suffered and died "so that by his death he might break the power of him who holds the power of death—that is, the devil—and free those who all their lives were held in slavery by their fear of death" (Hebrews 2:14-15). We are not offering some soothing words to ease the pain of death and dying, words with no foundation in reality, such as saying "It's all right" when in reality things could not be worse. We are talking about a real and decisive victory over death, by which its power is broken. A new attitude to death and dying is possible because a new situation has dawned. *Read 1 Corinthians 15:1-28.*

---

1. Paul says that the death and resurrection of Christ are "of first importance" (v. 3). What reasons does this passage offer for why they are so important?

---

2. Verse 3 puts forward the essential reason why Jesus was crucified. What difference has his death meant for you personally?

---

3. Why was Paul extraordinarily grateful for the grace of God (vv. 7-11)?

---

4. What evidences does Paul offer that Jesus really rose from the dead (vv. 3-8)?

5. Verses 2 and 12-19 make bold statements about the implications if Jesus did not really rise from the dead. If he did not actually rise, what would change for the human race? For you personally?

6. What hope does the resurrection of Jesus offer to those who are afraid of death?

7. Taken together, verses 19-20 are like a great bridge spanning the gap from despair to hope. When have you experienced crossing such a bridge to hope because of Christ's resurrection?

8. How does Jesus' resurrection connect with the rest of humanity (vv. 20-23)?

9. What do verses 24-28 promise about the final victory of God?

10. Taken as a whole, what does this Scripture passage say to you about suffering here and now?

11. Consider specific difficult situations in your life. How does the resurrection of Jesus change your perspective on those circumstances?

Pray that you will grow in hope because Christ rose from the dead and lives today.

Now or Later

- Study the rest of Paul's development of the theme of resurrection in 1 Corinthians 15:29-58.

- To get a sense of the importance of Christ's death and resurrection in the earliest preaching of the apostles, study Acts 2:22-36.

- To rekindle your memory of the events named in this part of the creed, re-read the four Gospel accounts of Jesus' crucifixion and resurrection. Read one account per day for four days, or read all four in one sitting. What details had you forgotten? What details were somewhat different from what you remembered? What parts hold special significance for you right now?

5

God the Son: His Present Activity and Future Role; God the Holy Spirit

Colossians 1:15-20; 1 Corinthians 12:1-11

He ascended into heaven and is seated at the right hand of the Father. He will come again to judge the living and the dead. I believe in the Holy Spirit . . .

Jesus came to earth from heaven in great humility; he returned to heaven in triumph and glory, having accomplished all that was necessary for salvation. Yet in no way does the ascension of Christ mean that he is now *absent* from his world. Through the resurrection, Christ broke down the barriers of time and space, allowing himself to be available to all. The ascended Christ lives in believers through the Holy Spirit. We must not allow the limitations of our reason and imagination to impose restrictions on what the risen and exalted Christ can do.

GROUP DISCUSSION. Christians think a lot about what Jesus has done (dying and rising for us) and what he will do (return in glory). Why do we spend less time considering what Jesus is doing now in his ascended position at the Father's right hand?

PERSONAL REFLECTION. Do you feel that Jesus is more involved in some areas of your life than other areas? What are the areas you feel he is less involved in, and why?

The doctrine of the ascension assures us that Christ has been exalted and glorified, and that his power and glory can be revealed and reflected in our lives. The creed states that Jesus now sits at the right hand of God. This suggests special favor and status, and it suggests that Jesus has the Father's ear. *Read Colossians 1:15-20.*

1. How many times does the word *all* occur in this passage?

What do the various uses of *all* say to you about Christ?

2. Continue to meditate on Christ as portrayed in this Scripture. What are some fitting ways to worship such a person?

3. The creed states that Jesus "will come again to judge the living and the dead." Based on what you read in Colossians 1:15-20, what qualifies Jesus to judge humanity?

4. What thoughts and feelings come to you when you think about the fact that Christ will return?

---

5. All things were created in the Son, through him and for him (v. 16). What does the rest of this Scripture have to say about how the Son continues to be involved with his creation?

---

6. How do you respond to the idea that you personally were created for Christ?

---

7. What is Christ's relationship with the church—that is, those who believe in him (v. 18)?

---

8. We may sometimes feel that the world or even our own lives are falling apart. What difference does it make to know that in Christ "all things hold together" (v. 17)?

Read 1 Corinthians 12:1-11.

---

9. The creed states "I believe in the Holy Spirit." How do you see the Holy Spirit active in your church fellowship?

10. How do you see the Holy Spirit active in your own life?

11. How will this study affect you the next time you worship, whether privately or publicly?

Pray for greater sensitivity to the Holy Spirit's prompting in your life and in the life of your church fellowship.

Now or Later

- Study Jesus' words about judgment in John 5:19-30.
- The creed states that Jesus "is seated at the right hand of the Father." Study the scriptural basis for this statement:
  - Psalm 110:1: quoted by Jesus in Matthew 22:41-46; Mark 12:35-37; Luke 20:41-44; quoted by Peter in Acts 2:33-36; and quoted by the writer of Hebrews in Hebrews 1:13
  - Matthew 26:63-66 and Mark 14:61-64, where Jesus applies Psalm 110:1 to himself, sealing the charge of blasphemy
  - Ephesians 1:18-23

6

The Church, Forgiveness and Eternal Life

Ephesians 4:1-13

. . . the holy catholic church, the communion of saints, the forgiveness of sins, the resurrection of the body, and the life everlasting. Amen.

To believe in Jesus Christ is to believe in and belong to a dynamic community that spans the centuries. The Greek word *ekklesia*, used in the New Testament to refer to the church, denotes not a building but a group of people. It literally means "those who are called out." The church is not a static building but a dynamic pilgrim people who are constantly moving on in faith and obedience. It includes those who have gone ahead of us and those who will follow. It is a great fellowship of faith, spanning the ages and the continents.

GROUP DISCUSSION. Identify as many things as possible that your church has in common with Christians of other denominations or fellowship groups. Consider both inward beliefs and outward practices. Do the results of your informal survey surprise you?

PERSONAL REFLECTION. What are your attitudes toward Christians who belong to denominations different from yours? Which aspects of your beliefs and their beliefs feel most divisive, and which feel most unifying?

When the Apostles' Creed uses the term *catholic*, it means "according to the whole" or "universal." In saying that the church is catholic we affirm that its message is valid and relevant to every age and every situation. In several of his letters, Paul wrote of Christians' essential unity that underlies a diversity of gifts for service. *Read Ephesians 4:1-13.*

1. According to this Scripture, what do all Christian believers have in common? Find as many responses as possible.

2. What are some practical ways that Christians can "keep the unity of the Spirit through the bond of peace" (v. 3)? Consider not only theoretical ways but ways you have seen this actually happen.

3. After building a strong case for unity in verses 1-6, Paul abruptly switches to ways Christians differ (vv. 7-11). According to this Scripture, how are Christians dissimilar even in unity?

4. What is the relationship between Jesus' incarnation and his granting of gifts to his people (vv. 7-10)?

5. How does this Scripture passage express what the Apostles' Creed calls "the communion of saints"?

6. The creed expresses belief in "the forgiveness of sins" with no attempt to explain the idea or elaborate on it. Where in this Scripture passage do you see the idea of reconciliation between God and human beings?

7. How do the various gifts of service named in verse 11 contribute to the unity of the church?

8. Christ ascended in triumph (vv. 7-10) and lives forever. What different perspective on life can believers have because of the certainty, as the creed expresses, of "the life everlasting"?

9. What will be the ultimate result of Christians' gifts working together (vv. 12-13)?

10. How would you describe maturity in Christ (v. 13)?

11. As you look back on these six studies, what new insights have you gained about the Apostles' Creed and the faith it expresses?

12. Where would you like to deepen your understanding of the beliefs expressed in the creed?

Pray that your God-given gifts of service will be used to build up Christ's church.

Now or Later

- Study 1 Corinthians 14 concerning spiritual gifts and how they function to edify the church.

- Write a message of appreciation to someone whose spiritual gifts have blessed and helped you. If the person is no longer living, write the message as a prayer of thanksgiving for how the person's influence is still with you.

- Christians of many traditions and denominations regularly recite the Apostles' Creed in worship. The English wording of the creed varies somewhat across different translations. Read as many versions as you can find; church hymnals and orders of worship are a good source. What new insights do you gain by comparing different versions of the creed?

Leader's Notes

Leading a Bible discussion can be an enjoyable and rewarding experience. But it can also be *scary*—especially if you've never done it before. If this is your feeling, you're in good company. When God asked Moses to lead the Israelites out of Egypt, he replied, "Please send someone else" (Ex 4:13)! It was the same with Solomon, Jeremiah and Timothy, but God helped these people in spite of their weaknesses, and he will help you as well.

You don't need to be an expert on the Bible or a trained teacher to lead a Bible discussion. The idea behind these inductive studies is that the leader guides group members to discover for themselves what the Bible has to say. This method of learning will allow group members to remember much more of what is said than a lecture would.

These studies are designed to be led easily. As a matter of fact, the flow of questions through the passage from observation to interpretation to application is so natural that you may feel that the studies lead themselves. This study guide is also flexible. You can use it with a variety of groups—student, professional, neighborhood or church groups. Each study takes forty-five to sixty minutes in a group setting.

There are some important facts to know about group dynamics and encouraging discussion. The suggestions listed below should enable you to effectively and enjoyably fulfill your role as leader.

Preparing for the Study

1. Ask God to help you understand and apply the passage in your own life. Unless this happens, you will not be prepared to lead others. Pray too for the various members of the group. Ask God to open your hearts to the message of his Word and motivate you to action.

2. Read the introduction to the entire guide to get an overview of the entire book and the issues that will be explored.

3. As you begin each study, read and reread the assigned Bible passage to familiarize yourself with it.

4. This study guide is based on the New International Version of the Bible. It will help you and the group if you use this translation as the basis for your study and discussion.

5. Carefully work through each question in the study. Spend time in meditation and reflection as you consider how to respond.

6. Write your thoughts and responses in the space provided in the study guide. This will help you to express your understanding of the passage clearly.

7. It might help to have a Bible dictionary handy. Use it to look up any unfamiliar words, names or places. (For additional help on how to study a passage, see chapter five of *How to Lead a LifeBuilder Study,* IVP, 2018.)

8. Consider how you can apply the Scripture to your life. Remember that the group will follow your lead in responding to the studies. They will not go any deeper than you do.

9. Once you have finished your own study of the passage, familiarize yourself with the leader's notes for the study you are leading. These are designed to help you in several ways. First, they tell you the purpose the study guide author had in mind when writing the study. Take time to think through how the study questions work together to accomplish that purpose. Second, the notes provide you with additional background information or suggestions on group dynamics for various questions. This information can be useful when people have difficulty understanding or answering a question. Third, the leader's notes can alert you to potential problems you may encounter during the study.

10. If you wish to remind yourself of anything mentioned in the leader's notes, make a note to yourself below that question in the study.

Leading the Study

1. Begin the study on time. Open with prayer, asking God to help the group to understand and apply the passage.

2. Be sure that everyone in your group has a study guide. Encourage the group to prepare beforehand for each discussion by reading the introduction to the guide and by working through the questions in the study.

3. At the beginning of your first time together, explain that these studies are meant to be discussions, not lectures. Encourage the members of the group to participate. However, do not put pressure on those who may be hesitant to speak during the first few sessions. You may want to suggest the following guidelines to your group.

☐ Stick to the topic being discussed.

☐ Your responses should be based on the verses that are the focus of the discussion and not on outside authorities such as commentaries or speakers.

☐ These studies focus on a particular passage of Scripture. Only rarely should you refer to other portions of the Bible. This allows for everyone to participate in in-depth study on equal ground.

☐ Anything said in the group is considered confidential and will not be discussed outside the group unless specific permission is given to do so.

☐ We will listen attentively to each other and provide time for each person present to talk.

☐ We will pray for each other.

4. Have a group member read the introduction at the beginning of the discussion.

5. Every session begins with a group discussion question. The question or activity is meant to be used before the passage is read. The question introduces the theme of the study and encourages group members to begin to open up. Encourage as many members as possible to participate, and be ready to get the discussion going with your own response.

This section is designed to reveal where our thoughts or feelings need to be transformed by Scripture. That is why it is especially important not to read the passage before the discussion question is asked. The passage will tend to color the honest reactions people would otherwise give because they are, of course, supposed to think the way the Bible does.

You may want to supplement the group discussion question with an icebreaker to help people to get comfortable. See the community section of the *Small Group Starter Kit* (IVP, 1995) for more ideas.

You also might want to use the personal reflection question with your group. Either allow a time of silence for people to respond individually or discuss it together.

6. Have a group member (or members if the passage is long) read aloud the passage to be studied. Then give people several minutes to read the passage again silently so that they can take it all in.

7. Question 1 will generally be an overview question designed to briefly survey the passage. Encourage the group to look at the whole passage, but try to avoid getting sidetracked by questions or issues that will be addressed later in the study.

8. As you ask the questions, keep in mind that they are designed to be used just as they are written. You may simply read them aloud. Or you may prefer to express them in your own words.

There may be times when it is appropriate to deviate from the study guide. For example, a question may have already been answered. If so, move on to the next question. Or someone may raise an important question not covered in the guide. Take time to discuss it, but try to keep the group from going off on tangents.

9. Avoid answering your own questions. If necessary, repeat or rephrase them until they are clearly understood. Or point out something you read in the leader's notes to clarify the context or meaning. An eager group quickly becomes passive and silent if they think the leader will do most of the talking.

10. Don't be afraid of silence. People may need time to think about the question before formulating their answers.

11. Don't be content with just one answer. Ask, "What do the rest of you think?" or "Anything else?" until several people have given answers to the question.

12. Acknowledge all contributions. Try to be affirming whenever possible. Never reject an answer. If it is clearly off-base, ask, "Which verse led you to that conclusion?" or again, "What do the rest of you think?"

13. Don't expect every answer to be addressed to you, even though this will probably happen at first. As group members become more at ease, they will begin to truly interact with each other. This is one sign of healthy discussion.

14. Don't be afraid of controversy. It can be very stimulating. If you don't resolve an issue completely, don't be frustrated. Move on and keep it in mind for later. A subsequent study may solve the problem.

15. Periodically summarize what the group has said about the passage. This helps to draw together the various ideas mentioned and gives continuity to the study. But don't preach.

16. At the end of the Bible discussion you may want to allow group members a time of quiet to work on an idea under "Now or Later."

Then discuss what you experienced. Or you may want to encourage group members to work on these ideas between meetings. Give an opportunity during the session for people to talk about what they are learning.

17. Conclude your time together with conversational prayer, adapting the prayer suggestion at the end of the study to your group. Ask for God's help in following through on the commitments you've made.

18. End on time.

Many more suggestions and helps are found in *How to Lead a LifeBuilder Study.*

Components of Small Groups

A healthy small group should do more than study the Bible. There are four components to consider as you structure your time together.

Nurture. Small groups help us to grow in our knowledge and love of God. Bible study is the key to making this happen and is the foundation of your small group.

Community. Small groups are a great place to develop deep friendships with other Christians. Allow time for informal interaction before and after each study. Plan activities and games that will help you get to know each other. Spend time having fun together going on a picnic or cooking dinner together.

Worship and prayer. Your study will be enhanced by spending time praising God together in prayer or song. Pray for each other's needs and keep track of how God is answering prayer in your group. Ask God to help you to apply what you are learning in your study.

Outreach. Reaching out to others can be a practical way of applying what you are learning, and it will keep your group from becoming self-focused. Host a series of evangelistic discussions for your friends or neighbors. Clean up the yard of an elderly friend. Serve at a soup kitchen together, or spend a day working in the community.

Many more suggestions and helps in each of these areas are found in the *Small Group Starter Kit.* You will also find information on building a small group. Reading through the starter kit will be worth your time.

Study 1. I Believe. Genesis 12:1-8; 15:1-6.

Purpose: To expand our understanding of what it means to "believe" in God.

Question 2. At this point Abraham did not have a theological statement of faith setting forth who God was. He knew only that God had spoken to him and that God had great plans for him not only in the short term but also far into the future. Based on this knowledge, Abraham obeyed and set out for an unknown destination. His bare-bones knowledge and experience were enough to put him on the road in obedience.

Question 3. A surprisingly large number of people who think of themselves as Christians never get further than accepting the truth of Christianity. They believe that God is there, but they have never met him. They believe that God is able to forgive sins, but they have never allowed God to forgive their sins. They believe that God is reliable, but they have never relied on him. In eighteenth-century America, people like this were called "halfway" believers. They are on their way to faith, but they have yet to arrive. For such people, "I believe in God" can mean little more than "I think there may be a God somewhere." The richness and depth of the gospel remains unknown to them.

Question 6. Faith is saying yes to God. Faith involves knowledge but cannot be equated with knowledge. It is not a cold and cerebral idea that enlightens the mind but leaves the heart untouched. Faith is the response of our whole person to the person of God. It is our joyful reaction to the overwhelming divine love we see revealed in Jesus Christ. It is the simple response of leaving all to follow Jesus. It is a decision, an act of will to trust God.

Study 2. God the Father. Isaiah 40:21-31.

Purpose: To more deeply trust our almighty Creator and Father.

Question 2. The doctrine of creation allows us to feel at home in the world. It reminds us that we, like the rest of creation, were fashioned by God. We are here because God wants us to be here. We are not alone but are in the very presence of the God who made and owns everything, and who is also a friend who knows us and cares for us. Behind the apparently faceless universe lies a person.

Still, there is a limit to what can be known about God from nature. Christianity points to the biblical record culminating in Jesus

Christ, especially his death and resurrection, as the supreme demonstration of the existence and character of God. The biblical witness to God both confirms and extends any knowledge of God available from nature. The ultimate demonstration of God's continuing concern for and involvement in his creation is his act of redemption in Jesus Christ. Creation is the theater in which the great drama of redemption is played out.

Question 6. The word *almighty* causes problems for some. It is helpful to consider several points. First, all power and authority in this world derive from God. Rulers, governments and Christian leaders all derive authority from God (Romans 13:1-2) and are responsible to him for the way they exercise it. Second, things that seem impossible to us are perfectly possible for God. The angel who came to Mary reminded her of this truth (Luke 1:37). It is very easy for us to underestimate God; the creed reminds us that he is able to do far more than we imagine. Finally, *almighty* does not mean capricious or whimsical. Scripture stresses the reliability of God; having made a promise, God stands by it (Psalm 19:7-10). The fact that he is almighty doesn't mean that he can or will suddenly change his mind about this. In his power and wisdom, God has chosen to achieve our salvation and has committed himself to us in this way.

Question 7. When the creed speaks of God, it means "the God and Father of our Lord Jesus Christ" (1 Peter 1:3). It is not dealing with some philosophical ideas of God but with the God who revealed himself in Scripture and supremely in Jesus Christ. It does not refer to some abstract idea about God but to the *living* and *personal* God whom Christians worship and adore. This enhances our approach to God in prayer.

Question 8. Most human fathers, despite their weaknesses and shortcomings, wish the best for their children. How much more does God desire the best for us! But every now and then a child may ask his or her father for something that is totally inappropriate. The father's failure to give this to the child does not mean that he did not hear the request or that he has ceased to care for the child. Rather, it means that his care and concern for the well-being of the child prevents him from fulfilling that request. He may give something else instead, something more helpful and appropriate. Perhaps we could say that God answers the prayers that we ought to have prayed!

Question 9. First, notice how often Scripture compares God to a human mother. The love of God for his people is often compared to the love of a mother for her child (Isaiah 49:15; 66:13). Second, the analogy of God as Father also indicates *what human fathers ought to be like.* The same care, compassion and commitment God shows toward us are meant to be reflected in the attitude of human fathers toward their children. Third, remember that the best way to think about God is to think about Jesus Christ. "Anyone who has seen me has seen the Father" (John 14:9). Think of the love, care and kindness you see reflected in the face of Jesus. That is what the love of God for you is like.

Study 3. God the Son: His Identity and Birth. Philippians 2:5-11.

Purpose: To allow the lordship of Christ to lead us into worship.

Question 1. The Apostles' Creed identifies a number of key beliefs that allow us to understand why Jesus matters so much to Christians. First, it identifies that Jesus is the "Son of God." Although all believers are children of God in some sense of the word, Jesus is singled out as the Son of God. In the creed, saying that Jesus is the "Son of God" amounts to saying that Jesus is God. It is obvious that the first Christians worshiped and adored Jesus Christ—a practice that continues today. If Jesus were just another human being, a creature like the rest of us, then the New Testament writers would be guilty of worshiping a creature! But Jesus ought to be worshiped and adored precisely because he is God.

The name *Jesus* literally means "God saves." *Christ* is a title, not a surname; strictly speaking, the name should be written as "Jesus the Christ." *Christ* is the Greek version of the Hebrew word *Messiah* (see John 1:41). *Messiah* literally means "the anointed one"—in other words, one who has been anointed with oil and therefore singled out by God as having special importance. The basic sense of the word *Messiah* is "the divinely appointed King of Israel." The Messiah was the long-awaited deliverer of the people of God, promised in the pages of the Old Testament.

Question 4. The creed makes explicit reference to the virgin birth. This belief is important for three reasons. First, it makes important connections with Old Testament prophecy (Isaiah 7:14; Matthew 1:22-23). Here, as elsewhere in his career, Jesus brings to fulfillment great Old Testament hopes. Second, it stresses that Jesus was divine by nature, not by adoption at a later date. Third, it provided an important defense against early Jewish opponents of Christianity who suggested that Jesus was the illegitimate child of Mary (possibly hinted at in John 8:41). Such hostile critics suggested that Jesus was the son of a Roman soldier, thus insinuating collaboration with the foreign army of occupation. The New Testament has a rather different—and much more exciting—understanding of who the real father of Jesus was!

Questions 10-11. The creed does not refer to Jesus as *the* Lord but as *our* Lord. Jesus Christ has the right to lordship over our lives. This amounts to a demand for personal obedience and loyalty to him as our Lord and Savior. It is possible to pay lip service to Jesus as Lord yet deny him as Lord by the way we act (Matthew 7:21-22). To recognize that Jesus is Lord is to seek to do his will. But Jesus Christ is not merely the Lord of our personal lives; he is also the Lord of the church. The church owes its faithful obedience to Jesus Christ and to no one else. The church cannot and must not substitute anything or anyone for Jesus. If the church ever loses its faithful obedience to its Lord, it has lost its life and its soul.

Study 4. God the Son: His Death and Resurrection. 1 Corinthians 15:1-28.

Purpose: To emphasize that Jesus' death and resurrection are central to the gospel.

Question 1. The reference to Pontius Pilate in the Apostles' Creed firmly anchors the creed to history. The gospel affirms that God himself entered into history in order to meet us and redeem us. God came down to meet us where we are, in time and space. The gospel is not just about *ideas*; it is about God *acting, and continuing to act,* in history.

Question 2. The gospel is not merely about the fact that Jesus died, nor even that he was executed, nor yet that he was crucified. He died *for us.* Christianity is about the astonishing and thrilling truth that he died in order that we might be forgiven. Paul makes a clear distinction between the *event* of the death of Christ and the *significance* of this event. That Christ died is a simple matter of history; that Christ died *for our sins* is the gospel itself.

Question 5. When the creed says that Jesus "descended to the dead," it is a statement that Jesus really did die. For the New Testament writers, Christ was not raised "from death" (an abstract idea) but "from the dead." The Greek term literally means "out of those who are dead." He did not merely seem to die; he really did die and joined those who had died before him. And in the glorious act of resurrection, God raised him from the dead!

Question 7. Try to imagine what it must have been like to watch Jesus die on the cross. His suffering seemed utterly pointless. Where was God in all this? It was enough to make anyone doubt whether God existed in the first place. All those doubts were resolved through the resurrection. The apparently pointless suffering of Jesus was revealed as the means through which God was working out the salvation of sinful humanity. God was not absent from that scene; he was working to transform it from a scene of hopelessness to one of joy and hope. God's love was *demonstrated*, not contradicted, by the death of his Son (John 3:16; Romans 5:8).

Study 5. God the Son: His Present Activity and Future Role; God the Holy Spirit. Colossians 1:15-20; 1 Corinthians 12:1-11.
Purpose: To become more aware of the presence of Christ in the world through his Spirit.

Question 2. Thinking about the ascension is a helpful way of making sure that our outlook on life is right. It helps us recall that our destiny does not lie on this earth but with the ascended Christ, who has gone ahead of us to prepare a place for us. He is waiting for us now. This gives us a new perspective on the chores of everyday life. It sets before us a vision that keeps us going. It is like an oasis in the desert—vital refreshment in the midst of the heat of life.

Question 3. Many people find the idea of judgment deeply threatening. Three points may be helpful. First, *we are judged by someone who knows us totally.* We need not fear a superficial judgment based on inadequate knowledge of us and our situation. We can be honest about ourselves with God in a way that is impossible with other people. Second, *we are judged by someone who is passionately committed to us.* The cross reveals God's love for us as well as his judgment on us. Jesus himself was condemned by biased judges, hostile crowds and an indifferent public prosecutor; we, on the other hand, will be judged by one who cares deeply for us and is sympathetic toward us. Third, *we are judged by someone we know and trust.* We are already judged by our attitudes toward Jesus. Thus we are not judged on the basis of something unknown but on the basis of our response to Jesus

Christ. We have already been judged and know the outcome of that judgment; what remains is the confirmation and enactment of that judgment. Only God can save—yet, on account of his divinity, Jesus saves. In the same way, only God can judge us—yet, on account of his divinity, Jesus judges us.

Question 9. The trinitarian structure of the Apostles' Creed is now completed. Having dealt with faith in God the Father and God the Son, the creed turns to the Holy Spirit. In the two languages of the Bible, Hebrew and Greek, the words for *wind, breath* and *spirit* are the same. Two ideas help us gain insight into the vitality of the biblical understanding of the Spirit of God. First, *the Spirit brings life.* Just as God brought Adam to life by breathing into him, so God is able to bring individuals and his church to life through his Spirit today. Second, *the Spirit brings power.* The Spirit of God is like the wind—an unseen force that acts upon things and people. The Spirit can be thought of as God in action.

Question 10. We have only enough space to hit the high points of the richness of the Christian understanding of the work of the Holy Spirit.

- *The Holy Spirit convicts us of our sin.* Jesus promised his disciples the continued presence and power of the Spirit after he had left them. The Spirit would convict the world of its guilt and sin, and convince them of the reality of judgment (John 16:7-11).

- *The Holy Spirit is a pledge of our salvation* (2 Corinthians 1:22). The basic meaning of *pledge* is "down payment" or "token of commitment." God places his Spirit within our hearts as a down payment: it demonstrates that we are his and promises that there is more to come.

- *The Holy Spirit is our Comforter.* As Jesus prepared to leave his disciples, he promised to send them a Comforter (John 14:25-26). The Greek word *parakletos* is usually translated as "comforter," "advocate" or "counselor." The Greek word for *comfort* can also bear the meaning "urge on" or "encourage to do greater things." The Spirit prods us, encouraging and empowering us to do things we otherwise would not and could not do.

Study 6. The Church, Forgiveness and Eternal Life. Ephesians 4:1-13.

Purpose: To strengthen our commitment to the fellowship of believers.

Question 3. The disunity of churches does not deny the fact that the church is one. There are many different churches or denominations, yet to the extent that these are genuinely Christian, they are all part of the one church. And the church's message is valid and relevant to every age. It is not as if there were one church with a message suited to the second century and another with a message suited to the twenty-first. The same church, throughout all ages and across the world, seeks to apply the same gospel in any situation it may happen to meet.

Question 5. To declare that we believe in "the communion of saints" does not mean that we believe in a holy club; it means that we believe in a holy God who has called us as individuals into a community, within which his work of renewal and regeneration can take place. *Communion* is the old English word for fellowship, and it identifies a key role of the church. Among its many functions the church is there to support its members. At one level it means "sharing joys and sorrows." But fellowship operates at another level as well, the level of material goods and wealth. It is a reminder of the need for mutual commitment within the Christian fellowship. The word *saint* just means "someone who is holy." Christians are holy not because of anything they are in themselves but because of the One who has called them. God's holiness can be reflected in our lives, even if we ourselves are sinners.

Question 6. Forgiveness of sins is perhaps the most powerful and familiar concept used to explain the significance of Christ's death and resurrection for believers. Forgiveness of sins may be regarded as a legal concept involving the remission of a penalty or debt. Whatever penalty was due for human sin has been fully met by the obedient death of Christ on the cross. Forgiveness is also closely related to the idea of reconciliation. Forgiveness is what is necessary for a personal relationship to be restored to its former state after a hurtful disagreement or misunderstanding. Our sin separates us from God. The creed, however, affirms a central and joyous insight of the New Testament—this barrier *can* be and *has* been broken down by God.

Question 8. The Greek language, in which the New Testament was written, has two words for life. One (*bios*) means "mere biological existence"; the other (*zoe*) means "life in all its fullness." What we are being offered is fullness of life (John 10:10), which not even death itself can destroy. We are not being offered an endless extension of our biological existence but rather a transformation of that existence. *Eternal* does not mean "throughout all time"; it means "outside time." *Eternal life* means life with God, outside the confines of space and time. Eternal life is not something that lies totally in the future. We can begin to experience it now. While eternal life in all its fullness is something we can only hope to gain in the age to come, we are able to gain a foretaste of it now. Eternal life is inaugurated, though not fulfilled, in our present life as believers.

Alister McGrath is the Andreas Idreos Professor of Science and Religion at Oxford University. He has authored many books including I Believe, The Passionate Intellect *and* Doubting, *all with InterVarsity Press, and coauthored* The Dawkins Delusion? *(SPCK, 2007).*

Dale and Sandy Larsen are writers living in Rochester, Minnesota. They have authored over thirty Bible studies, including more than ten LifeBuilder Bible Studies.